JOHN MERRILL'S l CHALLENGE WALK

BY

JOHN N. MERRILL

Maps and photographs by John N. Merrill

a J.N.M. PUBLICATION

1987

a J.N.M. PUBLICATION

JNM PUBLICATIONS,
WINSTER,
MATLOCK,
DERBYSHIRE.
DE4 2DQ

Conceived, edited, typeset, designed, marketed and distributed by John N. Merrill.

© Text and routes — John N. Merrill 1987

© Maps and photographs — John N. Merrill 1987

First Published — August 1987

ISBN 0 907496 50 4

Meticulous research has been undertaken to ensure that this publication is highly accurate at the time of going to press. The publishers, however, cannot be held responsible for alterations, errors or omissions, but they would welcome notification of such for future editions.

Printed by: Commercial Colour Press, London E7 0EW.

Set in Futura — medium and bold.

ABOUT JOHN N. MERRILL

John combines the characteristics and strength of a mountain climber with the stamina and athletic capabilities of a marathon runner. In this respect he is unique and has to his credit a whole string of remarkable long walks. He is without question the world's leading marathon walker.

Over the last ten years he has walked more than 60,000 miles and successfully completed ten walks of at least 1,000 miles or more.

His six major walks in Great Britain are —
Hebridean Journey .... 1,003 miles
Northern Isles Journey .... 913 miles
Irish Island Journey .... 1,578 miles
Parkland Journey .... 2,043 miles
Lands End to John o'Groats .... 1,608 miles
and in 1978 he became the first person (permanent Guinness Book of Records entry) to walk the entire coastline of Britain — 6,824 miles in ten months.

In Europe he has walked across Austria — 712 miles — hiked the Tour of Mont Blanc, completed High Level Routes in the Dolomites, and the GR20 route across Corsica in training! In 1982 he walked across Europe — 2,806 miles in 107 days — crossing seven countries, the Swiss and French Alps and the complete Pyrennean chain — the hardest and longest mountain walk in Europe with more than 600,000 feet of ascent!

In America he used the the world's longest footpath — The Appalachian Trail -2,200 miles — as a training walk. He has walked from Mexico to Canada via the Pacific Crest Trail in record time — 118 days for 2,700 miles.

During the summer of 1984, John set off from Virginia Beach on the Atlantic coast, and walked 4,226 miles without a rest day, across the width of America to Santa Cruz and San Francisco on the Pacific Ocean. His walk is unquestionably his greatest achievement, being, in modern history, the longest, hardest crossing of the USA in the shortest time — under six months (178 days). The direct distance is 2,800 miles.

Between major walks John is out training in his own area — the Peak District National Park. As well as walking in other parts of Britain and Europe he has been trekking in the Himalayas five times. He has created more than ten challenge walks which have been used to raise more than £250,000 for charity. From his own walks he raised over £80,000. He is author of more than seventy books, many of which he publishes himself. His next major walk — 2.400 miles — is down the length of New Zealand.

CONTENTS

Page No.

INTRODUCTION 1

ABOUT THE WALK 2

HOW TO DO IT 3

THE LANGDALE VALLEY & START OF THE WALK 5

NEW DUNGEON GHYLL HOTEL TO HARRISON STICKLE — 2½ MILES 7

HARRISON STICKLE TO STAKE PASS — 2 MILES 9

STAKE PASS TO ESK HAUSE — 2¼ MILES 11

ESK HAUSE TO SCAFELL PIKE AND BACK — 3¾ MILES 13

ESK HAUSE TO CRINKLE CRAGS — 3 MILES 15

CRINKLE CRAGS TO LANGDALE VALLEY — 4½ MILES 17

LOG 19

AMENITIES GUIDE 20

TRAIL PROFILE — 6,000 FEET OF ASCENT 21

BADGE ORDER FORM 22

EQUIPMENT NOTES 23

OTHER CHALLENGE WALKS BY JOHN N. MERRILL 26

OTHER BOOKS BY JOHN N. MERRILL 27

INTRODUCTION

My first introduction to the Lake District was rather a rude awakening, being sent to the Eskdale Outward Bound Mountain School. I was a very keen climber, and after soloing the 90 foot high school building my headmaster sent me to Eskdale to "learn how!" In the event it was a magnificent month's holiday in torrential rain! But I learnt the basic craft and the layout of the peaks. Ascending all the main mountains and camping under walls. Far from taming me I became even more determined to make a living out of the outdoors. As a result I often visit the Lakes to run up a few more mountains from different locations. More recently my wife and I have a lodge in Langdale to cement our love for the area.

Having written about and inaugurated many challenge walks, I am continually being asked for new ones. The Lakes were the next on my list and I began to cast around ideas in my mind. My aim, like my other challenge walks, has been to link together my favourite places and illustrate the variety of walking to be found. At first I selected Wastwater and the Pillar group but it wasn't challenging enough. I looked at other areas but nothing really gelled in my mind. All the time my mind kept thinking of Langdale and its peaks.

As a result, when we came to our lodge I made the ascents of all the peaks and Scafell Pike — now more than fifty times. Finally my mind was made up. A tough walk where care is needed in bad weather but a fell walk that can only be rated as one of the finest in England. Having walked it all in sections I waited for good weather and on May 7th, instead of voting, was on my route from the Great Langdale Campsite. Ahead were about sixteen miles and more than 6,000 feet of ascent over ten peaks. As I climbed Sickle Ghyll the mist clung around and tops were covered. But as the time progressed the sun burned through bringing about one of the finest and most perfect mountain days I have ever had in Lakeland. The views and clarity were exceptional. I ate my way through four bars of chocolate and wearing a T shirt and shorts was soon badly sunburnt!

Little after nine hours of steady walking I was back at the campground, delighted at the circuit. Here then is my favourite high level route in the Lake District. It is tough but a walk of exceptional grandeur. I can only hope that on your circuit you enjoy the same kind of matchless weather as I. Have a good walk and let me know how you get on.

HAPPY WALKING!

JOHN N. MERRILL.
Derbyshire. May 1987.

1

THE LANGDALE PIKES

ABOUT THE WALK —

The walk is a challenging one and in a short distance includes the ascent of many of the principal mountains of the Lake District. On a bright summer's day you will have no difficulty in finding your way round. But, in low cloud and rain the route is either best abandoned or completed by only the most experienced walkers well versed in map reading and compass work. It is not a walk to be taken lightheartedly for the weather can change suddenly and much of the terrain is rocky. You should be well prepared, carrying efficient proven gear and be wearing strong well broken-in boots.

Bearing in mind the seriousness of the route, the walk is of exceptional character and well within the reach of the average walker. The route is so devised that there are several oppurtunities to descend back to the Langdale Valley should the weather detriorate or one of the party find the going too tough. Always remember there is no shame in descending early. It is always better to be prudent than sorry. Where possible let someone know what you are doing and your expected time of return, allowing ample margin for ascending the hills slower than expected, especially towards the end.

With these words of caution, set off and enjoy one of the finest mountain circuits in England. Enjoy the distant views, the bold lines of the fells, the distant lakes, and the stunning splendour of the Langdale Valley. Regaining the valley floor after the walk you can sense a feeling of intense satisfaction at your performance and be proud to have achieved it.

HOW TO DO IT —

The whole route is covered by the Ordnance Survey Map — 1:25,000 Outdoor Leisure Map — The English Lakes — South Western area.

The walk is devised to be done in a single day, allowing between 8 — 12 hours. It is not a race and is simply a hard route to be enjoyed at your own individual pace. Because of the nature of the terrain and weather conditions there are many places where the route can be aborted with a direct descent back to the Langdale Valley. For those who complete the walk a special four-colour embroidered badge and signed certificate by John Merrill is available from JNM Publications. A master record of all who walk the route is also maintained by them.

The whole route has been carefully mapped, and you should have no difficulty in walking round in good weather. You should always carry the the 1:25,000 O.S. maps and be well versed in how to use a compass. Whilst the route follows well defined paths it is still advisable in misty weather to use your compass to ensure you are walking in the right direction.

The initial ascent to the summit of Pavey Ark via Stickle Tarn is the longest ascent of the walk. Once you have gained this height the remaining ascents are shorter and not so steep. The descent from Pike of Blisco at the end is a long one, especially after such a sustained route. The secret to completing the whole route is to adopt a steady pace and maintain it all day. Do not rush at the beginning and remember it is a long route and you will need reserves of energy to ascend Pike of Blisco from Red Tarn. The best way to ascend is to keep a slow but continuous rythmn. To stop frequently is to disrupt your momentum and upset you psycologically making the ascent take longer. Don't ponder "how far up it is", just keep going and you will be surprised how soon you get there! Rather than eat sandwiches it is better to eat quick absorbing energy food such as glucose tablets, Kendal mint cake, bars of chocolate, or nuts and raisins.

The walk can be abandoned along the route by descending to the Langdale Valley from near Harrison Stickle, Stake Pass, Angle Tarn, Esk House after the Scafell Pike ascent, and at Three Tarns after Bowfell. The times quoted for each section are what I took on the final run through the route and are included as a basic guide to the average time needed to complete each section.

* Lake District Weather Forecast for Walkers — operates continuously. Tel. Windermere (09662) 5151.

THE LANGDALE VALLEY & START OF THE WALK

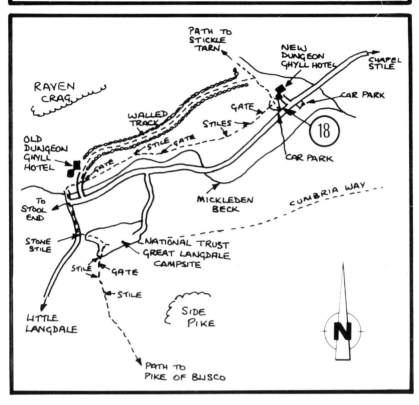

OLD DUNGEON GHYLL HOTEL

THE LANGDALE VALLEY AND START OF THE WALK

ABOUT THE SECTION — The walk basically starts from the car park beside the New Dungeon Ghyll Hotel. If you are staying locally you can park here and return here via the campground. If camping in the National Trust campground, you can walk over the fields to start.

WALKING INSTRUCTIONS — From the campsite walk to the western end of the site to a stone stile and footpath sign (those returning to the New Dungeon Ghyll Hotel will also come this way). Turn right along the road and keep straight ahead at the righthand corner and cross the Great Langdale Beck. Turn right through the gate to the kissing gate and road to Old Dungeon Ghyll Hotel.If heading stright on up the route to Stickle Tarn you can continue past the hotel on your left and follow the walled track to your right to join the starting out path just above the New Hotel. Those returning to the car park should, at the road after the kissing gate, go through the gate and cross the field to the far righthand corner to a wooden stile. Continue ahead to a gate and then onto two wooden stiles just above the beck. Over these keep ahead to a stone stile and in the next field pass a farm on your left, cross the farm track and gain a gate to enter the car park beside the New Hotel and Stickle Barn.

STICKLE GHYLL

NEW DUNGEON GHYLL HOTEL TO HARRISON STICKLE — 2½ MILES

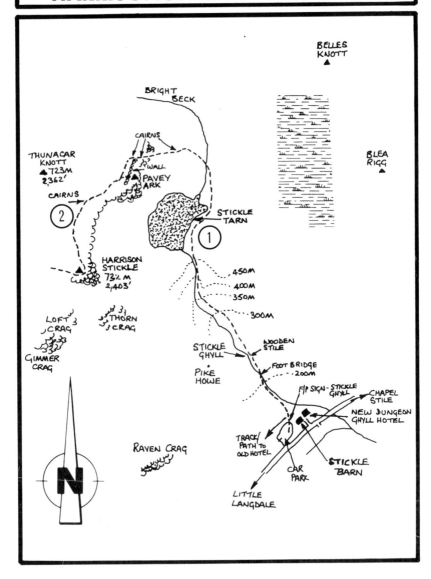

BELLES KNOTT

BRIGHT BECK

CAIRNS

THUNACAR KNOTT
▲ 723M
2,362'

WALL

CAIRNS

② PAVEY ARK

BLEA RIGG

STICKLE TARN

①

HARRISON STICKLE
73½ M
2,403'

450M
400M
350M

300M

LOFT CRAG

THORN CRAG

GIMMER CRAG

STICKLE GHYLL

WOODEN STILE

PIKE HOWE

FOOT BRIDGE - 200M

F/P SIGN - STICKLE GHYLL

CHAPEL STILE

NEW DUNGEON GHYLL HOTEL

RAVEN CRAG

TRACK/PATH TO OLD HOTEL

STICKLE BARN

CAR PARK

N

LITTLE LANGDALE

NEW DUNGEON GHYLL HOTEL TO HAR-RISON STICKLE
— 2½ MILES, 2,000 feet of ascent, allow 1½ hours.

ABOUT THE SECTION — The longest sustained ascent, first to Stickle Tarn where you get a short level section before ascending once more to the summit of Pavey Ark. A short gentle descent from here leads to the brief ascent of Harrison Stickle.

WALKING INSTRUCTIONS — Ascend to the top of the car park, with the hotel and Stickle Barn on your right. Go through the gate and past the path sign — Stickle Ghyll. Keep on the well defined path — now cobbled — and ascend Stickle Ghyll with the ghyll on your right at first to a footbridge. Across this continue ascending with the ghyll on your left to Stickle Tarn. Follow the path to your right close to the tarn's shore. After ¼ mile leave it on the path and soon cross Bright Beck near a cairn. You now ascend once more at an angle at first then straight up the well used rocky path, frequently cairned. At the top bear left close to a wall on your left and after a short distance over the stile on your left is the summit of Pavey Ark. Still keeping on the defined path across broken ground you descend slightly, guided by cairns, as you bear left and ascend to the summit of Harrison Stickle and its incomparable view of the Langdale Pikes.

SUMMITS FROM HARRISON STICKLE

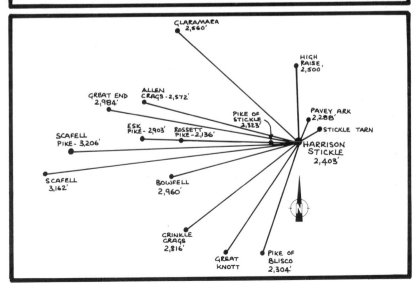

HARRISON STICKLE TO STAKE PASS — 2 MILES

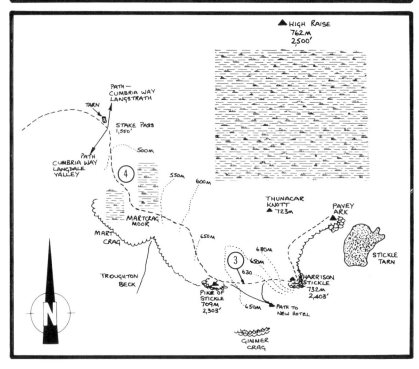

STICKLE TARN

HARRISON STICKLE TO STAKE PASS — 2 MILES — allow 1 hour

ABOUT THE SECTION — A short descent to the Dungeon Ghyll stream heads you towards the imposing summit of Pike of Stickle. A brief side trail leads you to the summit. From the fell you descend gradually over Martcrag Moor to the summit of Stake Pass close to a small tarn.

WALKING INSTRUCTIONS — From the summit of Harrison Stickle you follow the path westwards, descending to the infant Dungeon Ghyll. Over this you ascend to the righthand side of Pike of Stickle. On gaining its side a path to your left leads to its summit. Return the same way and follow the righthand path over the moor away from the valley edge, and soon begin descending Martcrag Moor. A little over halfway and it is quite boggy around several small tarns. Continue descending on the path to a cairn on the top of Stake Pass. Just ahead is the tarn, and your next path for Angle Tarn is just in front of it.

HARRISON STICKLE AND GIMMER CRAG

STAKE PASS TO ESK HAUSE — 2¼ MILES

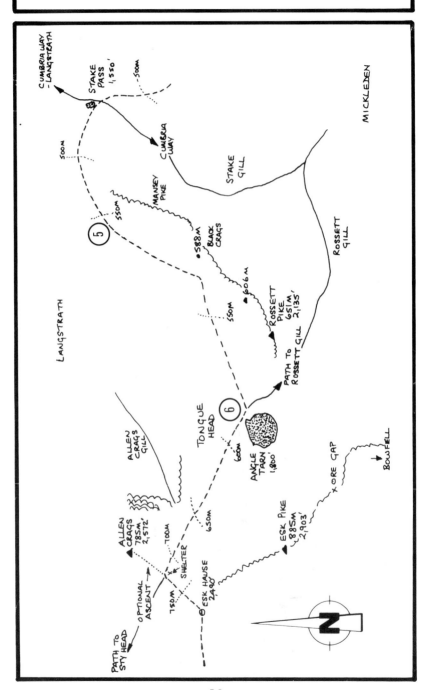

STAKE PASS TO ESK HAUSE — 2¼ MILES — allow 1¼ hours

ABOUT THE SECTION — You now begin the long and gradual ascent of Scafell Pike, heading first for Angle Tarn and then to Esk Hause. This is the point you return to after Scafell Pike for the continuation of the route to Esk Pike and on. As you near Esk Hause you have the option of ascending to the summit of Allen Crags. The whole section is along well defined paths, especially from Angle Tarn.

WALKING INSTRUCTIONS — Follow the path just in front of the tarn at Stake Pass. The path soon curves left as you ascend below the crest of the ridge on your left. After a mile you near a small saddle in the ridge below Buck Pike and here the path bears right, maintaining height to Angle Tarn. Turn right and follow the wide path as you ascend out of the basin and ½ mile later reach the footpath crossroads beneath Allen Crags and stone shelter nearby. Turn left to the cairns at Esk Hause, ten minutes away. To the left is the path up Esk Pike which you follow later. Ahead to your right is Great End, and crossing the broad shoulder of the ridge is the path for Scafell Pike. Esk Hause is the point you return to after ascending the Pike.

ANGLE TARN AND ESK PIKE

11

ESK HAUSE TO SCAFELL PIKE AND BACK —3¾ MILES

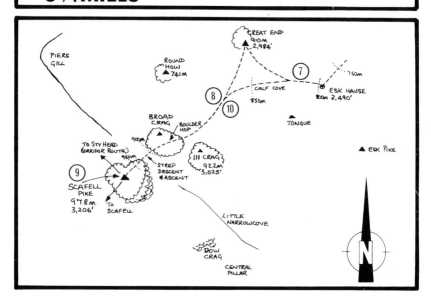

BROAD CRAG AND SCAFELL PIKE

ESK HAUSE TO SCAFELL PIKE AND BACK — 3¾ MILES.
— allow 1½ hours to summit and 45 mins for return.

ABOUT THE SECTION — The final ascent of Scafell Pike, England's highest mountain. Shortly after leaving Esk Hause you can ascend Great End before crossing broken ground over Broad Crag and on to Scafell Pike's summit. The path is well defined and cairned but quite rocky underfoot. The effort is worth it for the views are outstanding.

WALKING INSTRUCTIONS — Follow the cairned path across the broad ridge, and after a short distance you can bear right and follow a faint but cairned path to the summit of Great End, which provides good views of Scafell Pike. From the summit you can head towards Scafell Pike, picking up the route from Esk Hause which has ascended through Calf Cove. It is down this you will descend back to Esk Hause. The path is well cairned as you make your way over the many boulders beneath Broad Crag. A short descent follows to a saddle and the final ascent begins to the cairned summit of Scafell Pike. Retrace your steps back to Esk Hause.

SUMMITS FROM SCAFELL PIKE

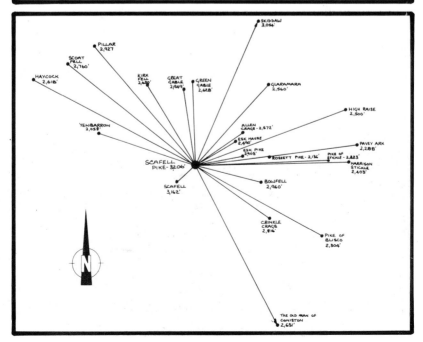

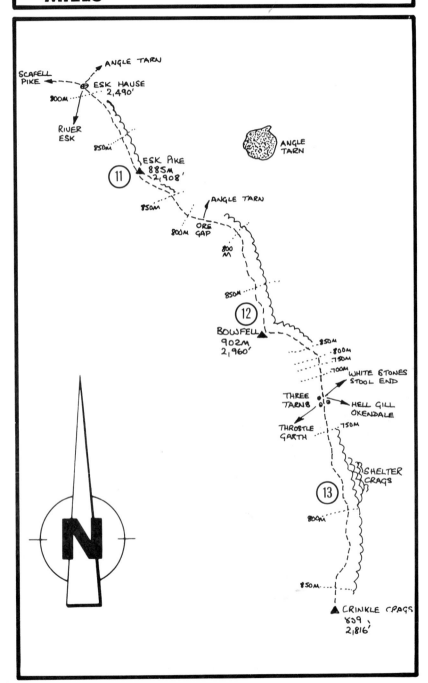

SCAFELL PIKE

ANGLE TARN

ESK HAUSE 2,490'

900M

RIVER ESK

850M

ESK PIKE 885M 2,908'

⑪

850M

ANGLE TARN

ANGLE TARN

800M · ORE GAP

800 M

850M

⑫

BOWFELL 902M 2,960'

850M
800M
750M
700M · WHITE STONES · STOOL END

THREE TARNS · HELL GILL OKENDALE

THROSTLE GARTH · 750M

⑬

SHELTER CRAGS

800m

850M

CRINKLE CRAGS 839 2,816'

N

ESK HAUSE TO CRINKLE CRAGS — 3 MILES
— allow 2 hours.

ABOUT THE SECTION — Back at Esk Hause you begin ascending again to the summit of Esk Pike and on to the summits of Bowfell and Crinkle Crags. Short descents from the summits of Esk Pike and Bowfell are followed by gradual ascents. It is a fine high level route with extensive views.

WALKING INSTRUCTIONS — Back at Esk Hause turn right and begin the short ascent on the distinct path up Esk Pike. You descend gently to Ore Gap and begin the ascent of Bowfell, whose summit is ¾ mile away. From this summit the path walks through a horizontal gully before turning sharp right and descending steeply to Three Tarns. The path keeps near to the ridge as you ascend to the cairned summit of Crinkle Crags.

ESK PIKE AND ORE GAP

15

CRINKLE CRAGS TO LANGDALE VALLEY —4½ MILES

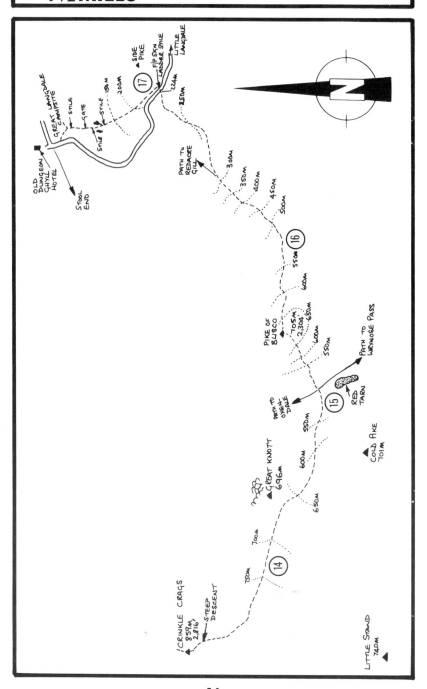

SIDE PIKE

F/P S/W
LADDER STILE

LITTLE
LANGDALE

225M

150 M

200M

350M

STILE

GATE

STILE

17

STILE

GREAT LANGDALE
CAMPSITE

PATH TO
REDACRE
GILL

300M

350M

400M

450M

500M

OLD
DUNGEON
GHYLL
HOTEL

STOOL
END

16

550M

600M

705M
2,304'

650M

PIKE OF
BLISCO

600M

550M

PATH TO
WRYNOSE PASS

RED
TARN

PATH TO
ONE-AL
DALE

15

550M

COLD PIKE
701M

GREAT KNOTT
696M

600M

650M

700M

14

750M

CRINKLE CRAGS
859M
2,816'

STEEP
DESCENT

LITTLE STAND
740M

16

CRINKLE CRAGS TO LANGDALE VALLEY — 4½ MILES.
— allow 2½ hours.

ABOUT THE SECTION — The final summit of the walk — Pike of Blisco — followed by a long descent to the valley where you began. Pike of Blisco is an ideal last summit for you can admire, with a sense of pride, all the peaks you have ascended on the walk. It is a moment to savour.

WALKING INSTRUCTIONS — The initial descent from Crinkle Crags is steep with a couple of scrambles. The path is well defined as you descend back into grass and moorland between Great Knott and Cold Pike towards the northern end of Red Tarn. Ahead is the imposing shape of Pike of Blisco and the ascent path can be seen quite clearly. From the cairn and nearby metal posthole begin the ascent to Pike of Blisco. The path from the summit is basically straight ahead as you traverse the mountain and begin descending the slopes of Wrynose Fell and on to Redacre Gill. The path is again well defined, and in the Gill watch for the path to your right, which you follow, as it basically contours round before descending to the summit of the road pass, beneath Side Pike. Cross the road, ascend the ladder stile and turn left as footpath signed and follow the path first close to the wall on your left to a wooden stile and through pine trees to another. Cross the subsequent field to a gate and more trees. Beyond is another stile where you enter the National Trust, Great Langdale Campsite.

LANGDALE VALLEY — OLD AND NEW DUNGEON GHYLL HOTELS AND GREAT LANGDALE CAMPGROUND

SUMMITS FROM PIKE OF BLISCO

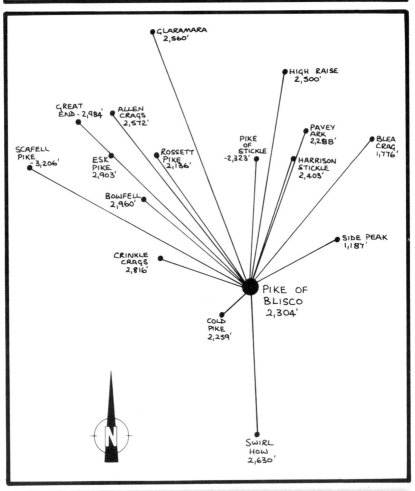

GLARAMARA
2,560'

HIGH RAISE
2,500'

GREAT
END - 2,984'

ALLEN
CRAGS
2,572'

PAVEY
ARK
2,288'

BLEA
CRAG
1,776'

SCAFELL
PIKE
- 3,206'

ESK
PIKE
2,903'

ROSSETT
PIKE
2,136'

PIKE
OF
STICKLE
-2,323'

HARRISON
STICKLE
2,403'

BOWFELL
2,960'

SIDE PEAK
1,187'

CRINKLE
CRAGS
2,816'

PIKE OF
BLISCO
2,304'

COLD
PIKE
2,259'

N

SWIRL
HOW
2,630'

RED TARN

18

LOG

DATE .... TIME STARTED .... TIME COMPLETED ...

| ROUTE POINT | HEIGHT IN FEET | MILE NO | TIME | | COMMENTS WEATHER |
			ARR	DEP	
New Dungeon Ghyll Hotel	363	0			
Stickle Tarn	1,525	1			
Pavey Ark	2,288	1¾			
Harrison Stickle	2,403	2½			
Pike of Stickle	2,323	3¼			
Stake Pass	1,550	4½			
Angle Tarn	1,800	6			
Esk Hause	2,490	6¾			
Great End	2,984	7½			
Scafell Pike	3,206	9			
Esk Hause	2.490	10½			
Esk Pike	2,903	11			
Bowfell	2,960	12			
Three Tarns	2,500	12½			
Crinkle Crags	2,816	13½			
Red Tarn	1,650	15			
Pike of Blisco	2,304	15½			
New Dungeon Ghyll Hotel	363	18			

AMENITIES GUIDE — in the Langdale Valley

VILLAGE	B&B	HOTEL	YHA	INN	CAMP	REST-AURANT	SHOP	P.O.
LANGDALE	*	*	*	*	*	*		
CHAPEL STILE	*	*		*	*	*	*	*
ELTERWATER	*	*	*	*		*	*	*

YHA & HOSTELS —

LANGDALE — Stickle Barn — next to New Dungeon Ghyll Hotel.

ELTERWATER — Youth Hostel, Elterwater, Ambleside, Cumbria. LA22 9HX Tel. Langdale (09667) 245

HIGH CLOSE — Youth Hostel, High Close, Loughrigg, Ambleside, Cumbria. LA22 9HJ Tel. Langdale (09667) 313

HOTELS — (Bed & Breakfast)

GREAT LANGDALE — New Dungeon Ghyll Hotel, Great Langdale,
Ambleside, Cumbria. Tel. Langdale (09667) 213

— Old Dungeon Ghyll Hotel, Great Langdale, Ambleside, Cumbria. Tel. Langdale (09667) 272

— Long House, Great Langdale, Cumbria. LA22 9JS
Tel. Langdale (09667) 222

— South View, Chapel Stile, Great Langdale,
Nr. Ambleside, Cumbria. LA22 9JJ.
Tel. Langdale (09667) 248

— Three Shires Inn, Little Langdale, Ambleside,
Cumbria. LA22 9NZ. Tel. Langdale (09667) 215

CAMPSITE — National Trust Great Langdale Campsite.

TOURIST INFORMATION CENTRE — Ambleside, Church Street,
Tel. 0966 — 32582

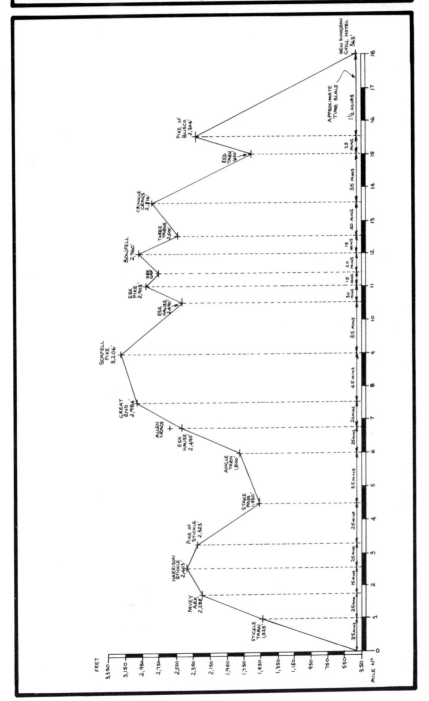

J M'S LAKELAND CHALLENGE

Badges are maroon cloth with figure embroidered in four colours and measure — 3" wide x 3½" high.

BADGE ORDER FORM

Date completed ....

Time ....

NAME ....

ADDRESS ....

....

....

Price: £1.75 each including postage, VAT and signed completion certificate.

From: J.N.M. Publications, Winster, Matlock, Derbyshire, DE4 2DQ
Tel: Winster (062988) 454 — 24hr answering service.

********* **You may photocopy this form if needed** ********

THE JOHN MERRILL WALK BADGE — walk this route twice or complete another John Merrill's challenge walk and send details and cheque/PO for £1.75 for a special circular walk badge. Price includes postage and VAT.

EQUIPMENT NOTES — some personal thoughts

BOOTS — preferably with a full leather upper, of medium weight, with a vibram sole. I always add a foam cushioned insole to help cushion the base of my feet.

SOCKS — I generally wear two thick pairs as this helps minimise blisters. The inner pair are of loop stitch variety and approximately 80% wool. The outer are a thick rib pair of approximately 80% wool.

WATERPROOFS — for general walking I wear a T shirt or shirt with a cotton wind jacket on top. You generate heat as you walk and I prefer to layer my clothes to avoid getting too hot. Depending on the season will dictate how many layers you wear. In soft rain I just use my wind jacket for I know it quickly dries out. In heavy downpours I slip on a neoprene lined cagoule, and although hot and clammy it does keep me reasonably dry. Only in extreme conditions will I don overtrousers, much preferring to get wet and feel comfortable.

FOOD — as I walk I carry bars of chocolate, for they provide instant energy and are light to carry. In winter a flask of hot coffee is welcome. I never carry water and find no hardship from doing so, but this is a personal matter! From experience I find the more I drink the more I want and sweat. You should always carry some extra food such as Kendal mint cake, for emergencies.

RUCKSACKS — for day walking I use a climbing rucksack of about 40 litre capacity and although this gives excess space it does mean that the sac is well padded, and has an internal frame and padded shoulder straps. Inside, apart from the basics for the day I carry gloves, balaclava, spare pullover and a pair of socks.

MAP & COMPASS — when I am walking I always have the relevant map — preferably the 1:25,000 scale — open in my hand. This enables me to constantly check that I am walking the right way. In case of bad weather I carry a compass, which once mastered gives you complete confidence in thick cloud or mist.

CRINKLE CRAGS AND BOWFELL FROM PIKE OF BLISCO

23

SCAFELL FROM SCAFELL PIKE

BROAD CRAG FROM SCAFELL PIKE

BOWFELL

REMEMBER AND OBSERVE THE COUNTRY CODE

Enjoy the countryside and respect its life and work.

Guard against all risk of fire.

Fasten all gates.

Keep your dogs under close control.

Keep to public paths across farmland.

Use gates and stiles to cross fences, hedges and walls.

Leave livestock, crops and machinery alone.

Take your litter home — pack it in, pack it out.

Help to keep all water clean.

Protect wildlife, plants and trees.

Take special care on country roads.

Make no unnecessary noise.

OTHER CHALLENGE WALKS BY JOHN N. MERRILL —

DAY CHALLENGES —

John Merrill's Peak District Challenge Walk — 25 miles.
Circular walk from Bakewell involving 3,600 feet of ascent.

John Merrill"s Yorkshire Dales Challenge Walk — 23 miles.
Circular walk from Kettlewell involving 3,600 feet of ascent.

John Merrill's North Yorkshire Moors Challenge Walk — 24 miles.
Circular walk from Goathland — a seaside bash — involving 2,000 feet of ascent.

The Little John Challenge Walk — 28 miles.
Circular walk from Edwinstowe in Sherwood Forest — Robin Hood country.

Peak District End to End Walks.
1. Gritstone Edge Walk — 23 miles down the eastern edge system.
2. Limestone Dale Walk — 24 miles down the limestone dales from Buxton to Ashbourne.

Forthcoming titles —

John Merrill's Peak District Challenge Walk No 2 — The Dark Peak Challenge.

John Merrill's Staffordshire Moorlands Challenge Walk.

MULTIPLE DAY CHALLENGE WALKS —

The Limey Way — 40 miles
Down twenty limestone dales from Castleton to Thorpe in the Peak District.

The Peakland Way — 100 miles.
John Merrill's classic walk around the Peak District.

The River's Way — 43 miles.
Down the five main river systems of the Peak District, from Edale, the end of the Pennine Way, to Ilam.

Peak District High Level Route — 90 miles
Circular walk from Matlock taking in the highest and remotest parts of the Peak District.

CRINKLE CRAGS

OTHER BOOKS BY JOHN N. MERRILL
PUBLISHED BY JNM PUBLICATIONS

DAY WALK GUIDES —

SHORT CIRCULAR WALKS IN THE PEAK DISTRICT
LONG CIRCULAR WALKS IN THE PEAK DISTRICT
CIRCULAR WALKS IN WESTERN PEAKLAND
SHORT CIRCULAR WALKS IN THE STAFFORDSHIRE MOORLANDS
PEAK DISTRICT TOWN WALKS
SHORT CIRCULAR WALKS AROUND MATLOCK
SHORT CIRCULAR WALKS IN THE DUKERIES
SHORT CIRCULAR WALKS IN SOUTH YORKSHIRE
SHORT CIRCULAR WALKS AROUND DERBY
SHORT CIRCUKAR WALKS AROUND BUXTON
HIKE TO BE FIT....STROLLING WITH JOHN
THE JOHN MERRILL WALK RECORD BOOK

CANAL WALK GUIDES —

VOL ONE — DERBYSHIRE AND NOTTINGHAMSHIRE
VOL TWO — CHESHIRE AND STAFFORDSHIRE

DAY CHALLENGE WALKS —

JOHN MERRILL'S PEAK DISTRICT CHALLENGE WALK
JOHN MERRILL'S YORKSHIRE DALES CHALLENGE WALK
JOHN MERRILL'S NORTH YORKSHIRE MOORS CHALLENGE WALK
PEAK DISTRICT END TO END WALKS
THE LITTLE JOHN CHALLENGE WALK
JOHN MERRILL'S LAKELAND CHALLENGE WALK

MULTIPLE DAY WALKS —

THE RIVERS' WAY
PEAK DISTRICT HIGH LEVEL ROUTE
PEAK DISTRICT MARATHONS
THE LIMEY WAY
THE PEAKLAND WAY

HISTORICAL GUIDES —

DERBYSHIRE INNS
100 HALLS AND CASTLES OF THE PEAK DISTRICT & DERBYSHIRE
TOURING THE PEAK DISTRICT AND DERBYSHIRE BY CAR
DERBYSHIRE FOLKLORE
LOST INDUSTRIES OF DERBYSHIRE
PUNISHMENT IN DERBYSHIRE
CUSTOMS OF THE PEAK DISTRICT AND DERBYSHIRE
WINSTER — A VISITOR'S GUIDE
ARKWRIGHT OF CROMFORD
TALES FROM THE MINES by GEOFFREY CARR

JOHN'S MARATHON WALKS —

TURN RIGHT AT LAND'S END
WITH MUSTARD ON MY BACK
TURN RIGHT AT DEATH VALLEY
EMERALD COAST WALK